An Anthology of Children's Animal Poems (A-Z)

alphabet poems for kids

Cam Wyllie

Illustrated by Indiah Morris

In loving memory of my mother GJ, the reason I'm here and for my love of writing and cooking.

To the love, strength & generous hearts of my children, Connor, Madison & Shaun who inspire me every day.

Andrew the Alligator

Andrew the Alligator was rehearsing his look,
The one he had seen in his reptile book.

Lying still as a log so as not to be seen,
Amongst all the bird life and lilies so green.

He was ever so good, never moving an inch,
Not even the rain, could make Andrew flinch.

The problem was with his enormous big smile,
He was the happiest gator on the long Blue Nile.

Always thinking of things that were silly and funny,
Jokes that were told by his best friend 'Billy Bunny'.

His mouth would turn up, to reveal his white pegs,
And the water would ripple from his paddling legs.

So Andrew the Alligator would always stand out,
He would grin and then laugh with even the trout.

The hippos and pelicans all thought him such fun,
In the comedy race he was number one.

While he tried as he might to catch his own prey,
His mum always gave him packed lunches each day.

Brad and Bob

Two busy baby bears walking hand in hand,
Browsing on the beach for bugs upon the sand.

Brad was brown and chubby with big blue eyes,
Bob was black and skinny and wore a bow tie.

Along the bay they travelled happy on their stroll,
Sifting out the beetles to fill their dinner bowls.

Bob began to bellow when Brad sat down to pause,
For the bugs and beetles scampered, down the sandy shore.

Brad said, 'I'm very sorry' and Bob said 'That's OK',
'It doesn't really matter on such a lovely day'.

'Let's head up to the mountains, where the breeze is nice and cool,
Perhaps we'll find some salmon swimming in a pool'.

So across the bridge they hurried, where the tall trees stood,
Up the sloping hills and through the friendly wood.

The fields were full of blossoms and bees amid the buds,
Brad was almost to the stream when Bob fell in the mud.

Now Bob was brown and sticky and he had lost his tie,
He was wet and cold and hungry, and then began to cry.

Brad said, 'Don't you worry, I'll catch you some fine fish',
'It will make you feel lots better, with supper in your dish'.

So both the bears had dinner and laughed about the day,
Then set out back for home, skipping all the way!

Camels

Ten crazy camels kicking cans across the sand,
Up and down the dunes, through the barren land.

Curious furry critters, with mounds upon their backs,
Each with one or two, except for poor old Max.

Max was never worried, about his lack of humps,
He always thought it better, not to carry round those lumps.

When all the other camels, would go to sleep at night,
They could only rest themselves to the left or right.

Max would lie upon his back with legs towards the sky,
He could watch the twinkling stars, shining up so high.

The tails the other camels had, were very short and stiff,
Max's tail was very long and flicked around in wisps.

He would much prefer to chew, upon a bale of hay,
Than to stand beside the water, drinking half the day.

It would seem that Max is not, your normal Arab camel,
He looks much more like, another kind of mammal.

Can you guess his name, I'm sure you can of course,
Max is not a camel, he is in fact a horse!

Dolphin Water Polo

A dozen darting dolphins flipping on the sea,
Diving 'neath the waves, swimming with such glee.

'Let's play a game of polo', Desmond said to Paul,
'We'll pick a team of six, with a buoy for a ball'.

'As we have two families here, six in each is great,
Greys against the Speckles and play until it's late'.

'I found some string for nets' said little Johnny Kleggs,
Al and Pete can make the goals between their many legs.

Al was an inky octopus, and Pete a giant squid,
The referee was easy, a Killer Whale called Sid.

The seals were on the sideline cheering on the Greys,
Hoping they would win before the end of day.

Electric eels were lighting up, to show the crowd the score,
Grey's had scored just three and the Speckled were on four.

Half-time in the ocean, so the dolphins got a rest,
It was going to be a struggle, to find out who was best.

The Grey ones swam out first, hoping for a win,
On came Steve the Stingray with his enormous wings.

The ball was flicked about, by fins and nose and tail,
Until it came to Steve, always scoring without fail.

A victory for the Greys, of which the fish approved,
When Steven came to help, it was rare for them to lose.

Ernie the Egg

Ernie was a tiny egg who had fallen out his nest,
He had a pair of little legs and a brightly coloured vest.

He roamed across the fields looking for his home,
A very brave, baby bird, not afraid to be alone.

Bumping into several trees whilst looking for his Mum,
All the nests were up so high, and this made Ernie glum.

'I'll never find my mother, whilst I am this far down,
Some wings are what I need to get me off the ground'.

Just then Ernie's shell, began to show some cracks,
Out came feathered wings, of speckled white and black.

Ernie flew up to the branches to see what he could spy,
The problem was he couldn't see, without the use of eyes.

So Ernie with his wings, tapped out some little gaps,
This meant that he could see, as well as he could flap.

Another crack began to grow, underneath his eyes,
Out came a shiny beak, so he could squawk and cry.

Flying round in circles, well above the trees,
The little bird was chirping, flying with such ease.

Then he heard his mother, shouting out his name,
She was with his brothers, all looking much the same.

Ernie's Mum was very happy, that he had been returned,
She wrapped her wings around him, and fed to him a worm.

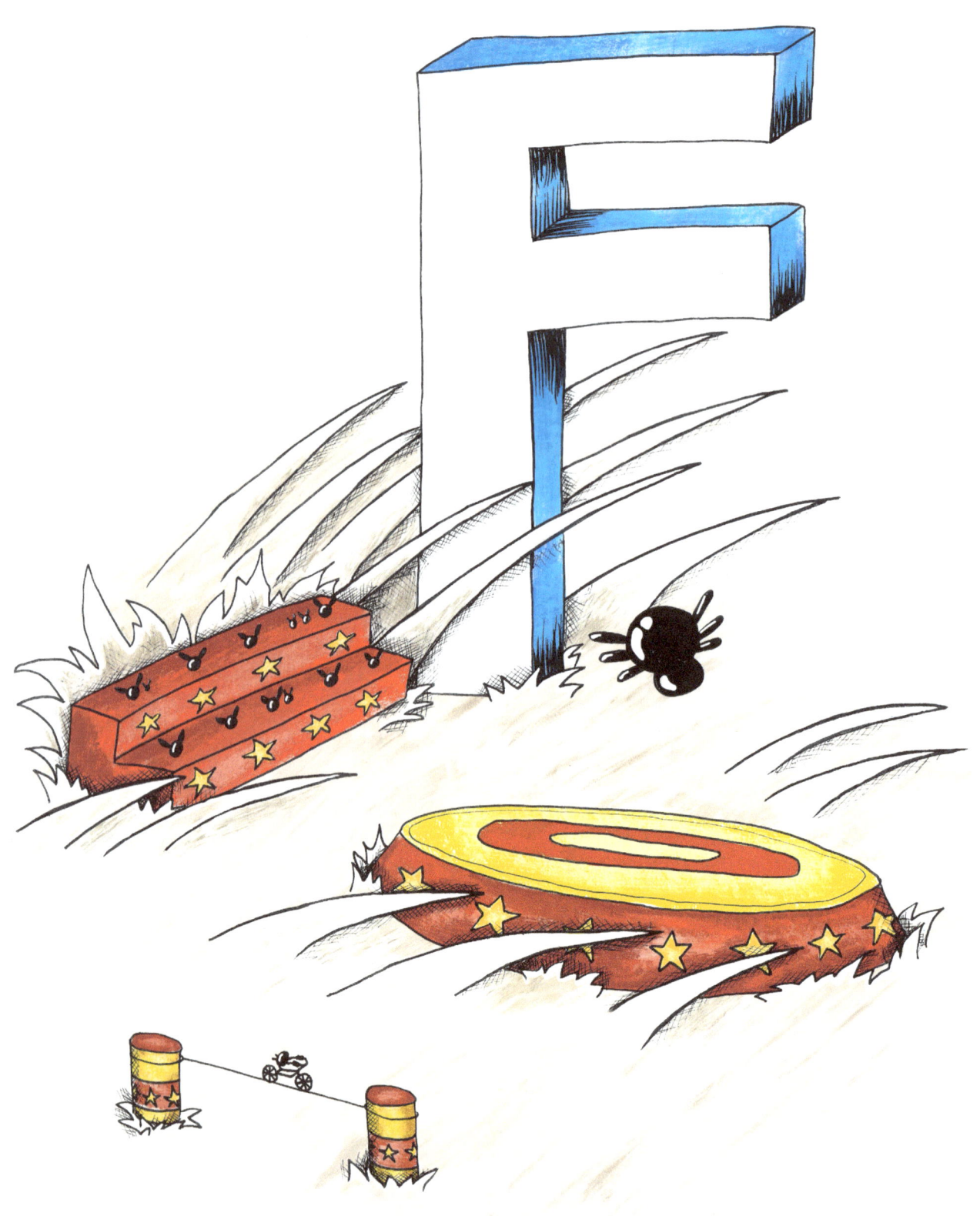

Flea Circus

The children sat down quietly to watch the evening show,
Each night at half past six, on the back of Billie-Joe.

Billie-Joe was not aware, he had a circus near his tail,
A group of fine young fleas appearing without fail.

The fleas were fearless flyers on the high trapeze,
Each waiting for their go, taking turns in threes.

All the kids would clap, at every catch and throw,
But the noise would never wake, the sleeping Billie-Joe.

Across the tiny tightrope the daring fleas would roll,
Some on little bicycles, some with just a pole.

The action often centred, around the middle ring,
Where Fred was found to show off, his ability to spring.

He could jump a good deal higher, than any of the rest,
Even if they had with a trampoline, Fred was still the best.

There was only one small problem, just a little catch,
If they ran around too much, this caused the dog to scratch.

When Billie-Joe was itching he would scatter all the fleas,
His wagging tail would stir up a mighty blowing breeze.

So all the fleas departed, and the children went to bed,
But they'll be back tomorrow, including our friend Fred!

The Great Race

At the edge of the jungle, the animals had come,
From wide and afar to watch the big run.

The race was between the giraffes and gazelles,
Monkeys were screeching and ringing their bells.

Baboons were preparing to judge in their chairs,
Wise, clever creatures that were always so fair.

An elephant trumpeted to signal the start,
The gazelles and giraffes sped off with a dart.

Birds flew overhead, up high in the sky,
Cheering the race with their loud noisy cries.

The gazelles were ahead, bounding quickly along,
But the giraffes still appeared to be ever so strong.

At halfway rock, it was the gazelles by a touch,
The giraffes were behind, but it wasn't by much.

The race nearly ended in a big dusty bowl,
Some zebras were crossing, to the watering hole.

With a pounding of hooves around the last bend,
There was nothing between them, nearing the end.

Stretched tight as a rope was a boa constrictor,
First past the snake, would be the race victor.

It was incredibly close at the end of their trek,
The giraffes bent down low and won by a neck!

Henry the Hornbill

Henry was a Hornbill, who lived among the trees.
He had a naughty side that pleased the chimpanzees.

The chimps would scream and shout and giggle with delight,
At the trouble Henry caused, each and every night.

With Henry's long sharp beak, he'd make anything he could,
Shaping different forms from the jungle trees and wood.

Henry slashed and sliced, until the morning sun,
Working long and hard, but always having fun.

When morning came each day there was always a surprise,
The chimps were clapping loudly and yelling happy cries.

He liked to fool them all, with things that looked quite real,
Made in the dark of night, for the morning to reveal.

A herd of drinking elephants, full of mighty power,
Causing all the real ones, to stand in line for hours.

An enormous roaring lion, snarling with his teeth,
Keeping every creature, at bay throughout the week.

But Henry's best impression, was of the other birds,
Particularly of Hornbills, so the chimps had heard.

The other birds would come, amid the shrieks and squawks,
Making sure that Henry, was never short of talk.

Ian the Iguana

In an ocean called Pacific, lies an island full of fun,
Where Ian the Iguana, spends days lazing in the sun.

He'd lie around on rocks, watching waves onto the shore,
To all the other animals, Ian seemed like such a bore.

What they didn't realise, was his ability to change,
Being any colour was weird and very strange.

Ian moved around a lot, he was very hard to see,
Staying in the background, blending with the trees.

He'd sit among the monkeys, watching with delight,
Itching, scratching, playing, in the bright sunlight.

Sometimes when he was angry, he would turn bright red,
Looking like a lobster, from nose to tail they said.

He could turn a speckled colour, lying very stiff,
In amongst the mushrooms, where the pigs would sniff.

When all the frogs were playing, croaking out their names,
They were unaware that Ian, was in the middle of their game.

So while the other animals, thought he just sat and stared,
Ian travelled lots and lots, but no-one saw him there.

Ian had some friends, also thought quite boring,
Can you count how many, are hidden in this drawing.

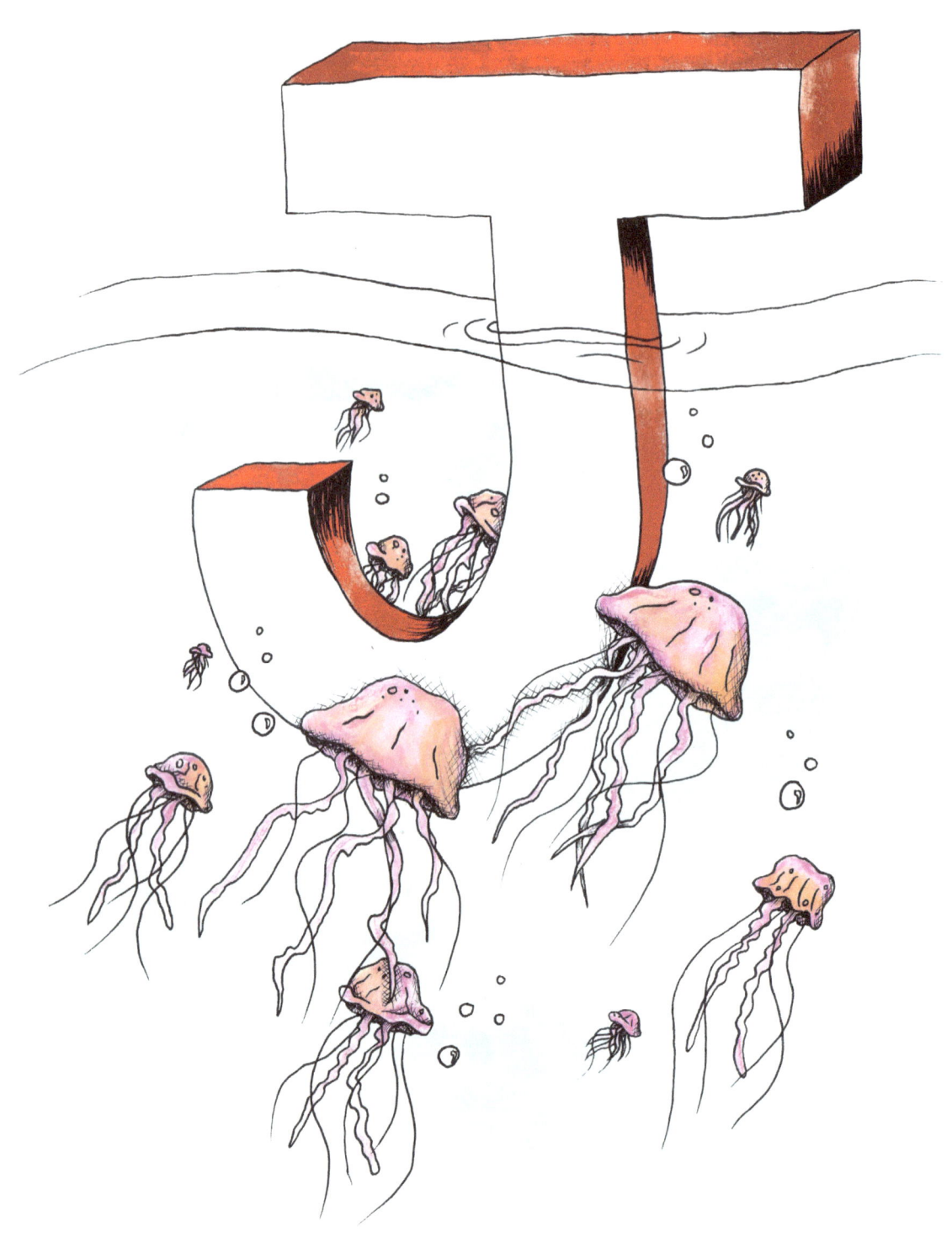

Jellyfish Jam

Two jolly jellyfish drifting with the tide,
Josephine and Jimmy, swimming side by side.

Floating on the waves, happy just to be alone,
With no-one else about, till along came Jack and Joan.

Four were not together, for very long it seems,
Next to join the flock, were Jonathan and Jean.

Six would turn to eight, as it began to rain,
Two more came long called Jeremy and Jane.

Julia and Jonah also liked the weather,
Ten jolly jellyfish cramming close together.

Twelve would make a dozen, underneath the clouds,
Jocelyn and Joe swam by to join the crowd.

As the sun broke through to show its golden rays,
The numbers came to fourteen with Jennifer and Jay.

Attracted by the others, in came Jill and Jake,
Now we're up to sixteen, if there's no mistake.

Jed and Joy made eighteen in an ever-growing group,
Just how many more, could fit into this troop.

Jellyfish Jam it looks like, by adding James and June,
Twenty jolly jellyfish, who has got the spoon?

The Koalas

Every night for their dinner, the koalas would feast,
But only on gum leaves were they able to eat.

One day the mother with the daughter went off,
To visit an Aunt in the bush way up north.

The father was left to get dinner for his son,
So the mischievous pair decided to have fun.

'Shall we taste the delights of a Wombat Ragout'
'Oh no' said the son, 'that will never quite do.'

'What about dingoes all covered in sauce?'
'Not for my stomach, they're as tough as a horse.'

'Then what about dining on Echidna Pie?'
'There's too many spikes to poke out my eye.'

'Well Kangaroo fritters I'm sure will taste great,'
'Come off it Dad, they'll jump of my plate.'

'Don't tell me you wouldn't, enjoy Platypus Stew.'
'You'll never find one, they're just far too few.'

'Goannas can be baked, roasted or fried,'
'I can't eat a lizard', the son did reply.

'We could barbecue steaks of Old Man Emu',
'He might be too tough for my small mouth to chew.'

'Then what would you like to fill up your tum',
'It's what I am served, each day by my Mum.'

'The Eucalypt tree provides all that we need,
Delicious and yummy, tasty gum leaves.'

Larrabe & Lil

In Peru, in South America way up in the hills,
Lives a pair of lively llamas called Larrabe and Lil.

Larrabe and Lil were always jumping in the air,
Happy laughing llamas without a single care.

Whilst skipping down a slope on a gloomy rainy day,
They found a woolly llama standing in the way.

Lionel was a bully who thought he was the best,
He wouldn't let you go, unless you passed a test.

You had to leap much higher than Lionel off the ground,
So he would let you travel, past his little mound.

Deciding to jump first, Lil leapt toward the sky,
But Lionel got up higher, he hardly had to try.

Larrabe was worried about his ability to win,
But Lionel was confident, and wore a massive grin.

Crouching down in readiness for the competition,
Larrrabe decided he should try a new position.

So that they could triumph, he tried a different tack,
Larrabe got Lil to climb up on his back.

All the woolly llamas then sprang up with a whoosh,
But as Lionel stopped rising, Lil gave a second push.

And with that extra leap, they had won the game.
Larrabe and Lil had achieved leaping llama fame.

Matt Mouse

In a musty mouldy manor, in a long-forgotten house,
There lived a lonely creature, a tiny little mouse.

Matt was not a shy mouse, in fact he loved a chat,
But all his friends had vanished, scared of Fats the cat.

Matt was most upset there was no-one else to play,
He sat and hoped and waited, each and every day.

But Fats was at the door to frighten off his mates,
A mean and nasty pussy and mice he loved to hate.

If Matt could find some friends who also weren't afraid,
They might just beat old Fats with a clever little raid.

The word went out to mice right across the town,
And soon there was a mob, outside the manor's ground.

Matt was thrilled his friends had come to help him out,
With such a lot of mice, they would win he had no doubt.

So they all sat down to listen after marching through a crack,
Matt explained his cunning plan to win the manor back.

First some sleeping powder, to pour in Fats' cream,
It wouldn't really hurt him, just enough to make him dream.

When Fats was fast asleep, the mice all gathered round,
And with a mighty effort, they pulled him off the ground.

They took him out the gate and down the winding road,
Then left him at the pet shop that belonged to Mrs Toad.

Early the next morning, some children purchased Fats,
They took him back to their house to chase away the rats.

The mice were very happy at winning back their house,
They cheered and clapped their hero, tiny Matt the mouse.

Nightingales

Nine noisy nightingales perched way up in a tree,
Singing all together full of fun and glee.

One saw a tasty worm and thought it time to munch,
Now there were only eight, since Ned had gone for lunch.

Nancy heard her baby squawk calling out her name,
She left to help the little chick, so seven did remain.

A flock above was heading south to beat the winter cold,
Six were still quite chirpy as Neville left the fold.

Five was all there were to sing, as Nova went as well,
Flying back to see her friends, followed soon by Nell.

The noise grew less but still they sung, even with just four,
Soon they shrunk again to three when Nick had left the core.

Noddy felt the need to leave and have a bath in dirt,
Two noisy nightingales, still carrying on the mirth.

The only way that Niles would go, was if it were to rain,
As soon as water fell from clouds, he left atop a train.

Natasha stayed upon her perch still chirping out her song,
All her friends would hear her sing and be back before too long.

Olly Octopus

Olly, Olly, Octopus, swimming in the sea,
Looking through my goggles, oh where can he be?

Olly, Olly, Octopus, down beneath the waves,
Is he hiding out, in the dark and gloomy caves?

Olly, Olly, Octopus, amongst the green seaweed,
Are those his dangly legs, looking like some reeds?

Olly, Olly, Octopus, on the ocean floor,
Can you see his eyes, through that old car door?

Olly, Olly, Octopus, in a wrecked ship,
Is that a little porthole or Olly's bottom lip?

Olly, Olly, Octopus, inside a giant clam,
Curling up like a pearl, annoyed by grains of sand?

Olly, Olly, Octopus, on a coral reef,
Watch him swim so carefully, will he come to grief?

Olly, Olly, Octopus, amongst the pretty fish,
Can he miss the angler's hooks, and avoid a supper dish?

Olly, Olly, Octopus, is always in the pink
He can be invisible, squirting out black ink.

Pono the Peacock

Peacocks are proud and love their fine tails,
The Peahens don't have any, it's only the males.

They use them to show off and attract them a wife,
Were a peacock to lose them, it would cause him such strife.

A young peacock called Pono, loved playing around.
Always getting in trouble with the things he had found.

Picking up objects in the fields and the parks,
Things that the kids left, behind in the dark.

One day when Pono was in search of some fun,
He saw something burning near some old burger buns.

Some humans were foolish and not put out their fire,
Having finished their food, cooked over some wire.

Pono brushed all his feathers on some smouldering stuff,
In an instant they vanished in a bright smokey puff.

Pono was sad and rushed back home to his Mum,
He was crying and crying at the sight of his bum.

His mother said 'Pono, try not to be blue',
'Go ask your father, what you should do'.

His Dad said, 'Let me look at, that horrible mess',
'I've got a novel idea' he had to confess.

A lady's fine fan with lots of colours and shades,
Stuck on with some glue and carefully displayed.

Pono smiled at his Dad, 'I look like a male!'
From now on he'd watch where he rested his tail.

Queen Bee

Hanging from the branches, in amongst the trees,
Are lots of lovely hives for busy honey bees.

The Queen was in her chamber sitting on her throne,
Shouting out her orders to all the worker drones.

Guards stood at the entrance, checking off the guests,
They were not allowed to let in, any naughty pests.

The workers buzzed about, then flew out of the hive,
Searching for sweet nectar that would keep Queen alive.

She sat and ate and ate, and then began to moan,
'You have to work much harder to fill my honeycomb',

Her crown began to slip, from her swollen head,
Then 'Crash' the legs were broken on her royal bed!

The bees kept working harder to try and please their Queen,
It seemed their bloated leader was intent on being mean.

Struggling with their heavy loads, to try and reach the door,
Wings were beating faster, much faster than before.

The Queen cried out 'More honey – you must give me more to eat'
'I want to scoff down honey, till I cannot see my feet!'

So all the bees flew off, to try and find some more,
Alas and woe when they came back, she had fallen through the floor.

The bees worked hard all through the night, to build another nest,
And now the Queen was sad, she couldn't help the rest.

They finished off a brand new hive, complete with glistening throne,
Down they flew to fetch their Queen, and fly her to their home.

She had learnt her lesson well, on how to help and care,
Whatever else you want to do, make sure you learn to share.

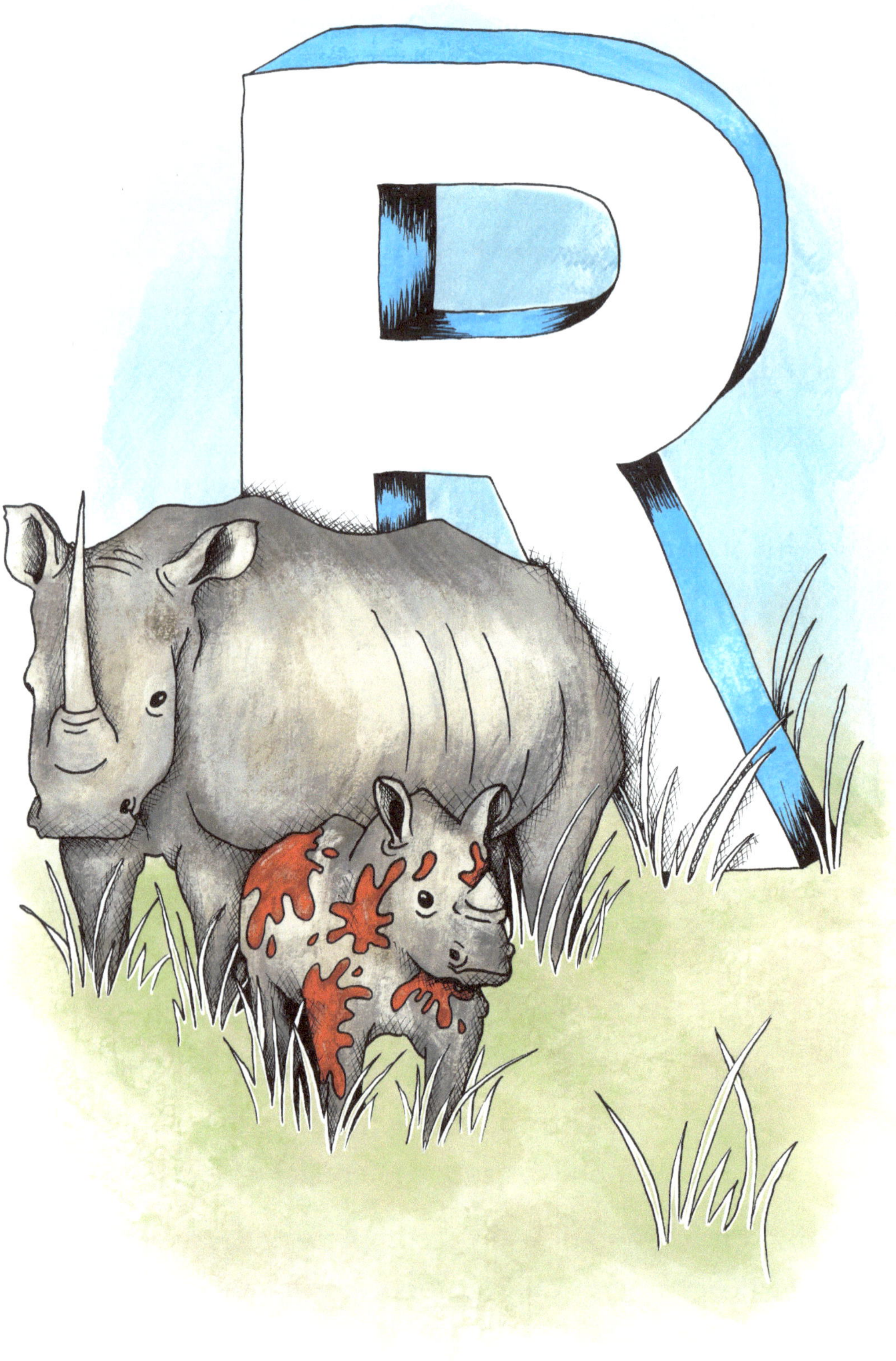

Reggie the Rhino

Reggie was a Rhino of very special fame,
His hide was red and fiery, like a brightly burning flame.

When he was just a baby, he had wandered into town,
He came across a circus, full of elephants and clowns.

In a yellow trailer, where all the clowns got dressed,
Reggie found a very smart, green and purple vest.

He put it on and then he found, a pair of floppy shoes,
These were far too large and bright, for anyone to use.

Next he thought, 'It's time for me to try and paint my face,
I have to think which one to use of all the pretty pastes'.

He looked at all the tubes and decided on the red,
Reggie tried to pick it up with the horn upon his head.

The paint began to leak and he began to cough,
Things got even worse as he tried to shake it off.

Red paint was flying everywhere all across the room,
Reggie turned from grey to red, in the afternoon.

Arriving home that evening, his mother got a shock,
Her baby boy was very red down to his little socks.

36

Stinky

In a green and wooded forest, underneath the bright sunlight,
There lives a little creature, whose fur is black and white.

Because he often left behind, a smell that was quite bad,
The others called him Stinky, since he was just a lad.

When the creatures gathered, to chatter or to drink,
They knew if he was there when it began to stink.

Stinky wasn't bothered, how the others treated him,
For he always had his pal, a Grizzly Bear called Jim.

The reason Jim was happy, to be around his little mate,
Was mostly due to hay-fever, that kept Jim in such a state.

He couldn't smell at all, through his blocked and reddened nose,
So he stayed by his pal Stinky, in times of high and low.

Then one day a hunter came, with his dogs and gun,
He aimed to shoot some creatures, beneath the setting sun.

Everyone was very scared, and scampered off to hide,
Only Jim was left in sight, with Stinky at his side.

The dogs began to bark, so the hunter saw the pair,
Stinky watched him raise his gun, and give an evil glare.

So stinky let him have it, his worst disgusting smell,
The dogs ran off and left their master, feeling most unwell.

After that Stinky found, he was treated like the rest,
Grizzly Jim announced, he had more than passed the test.

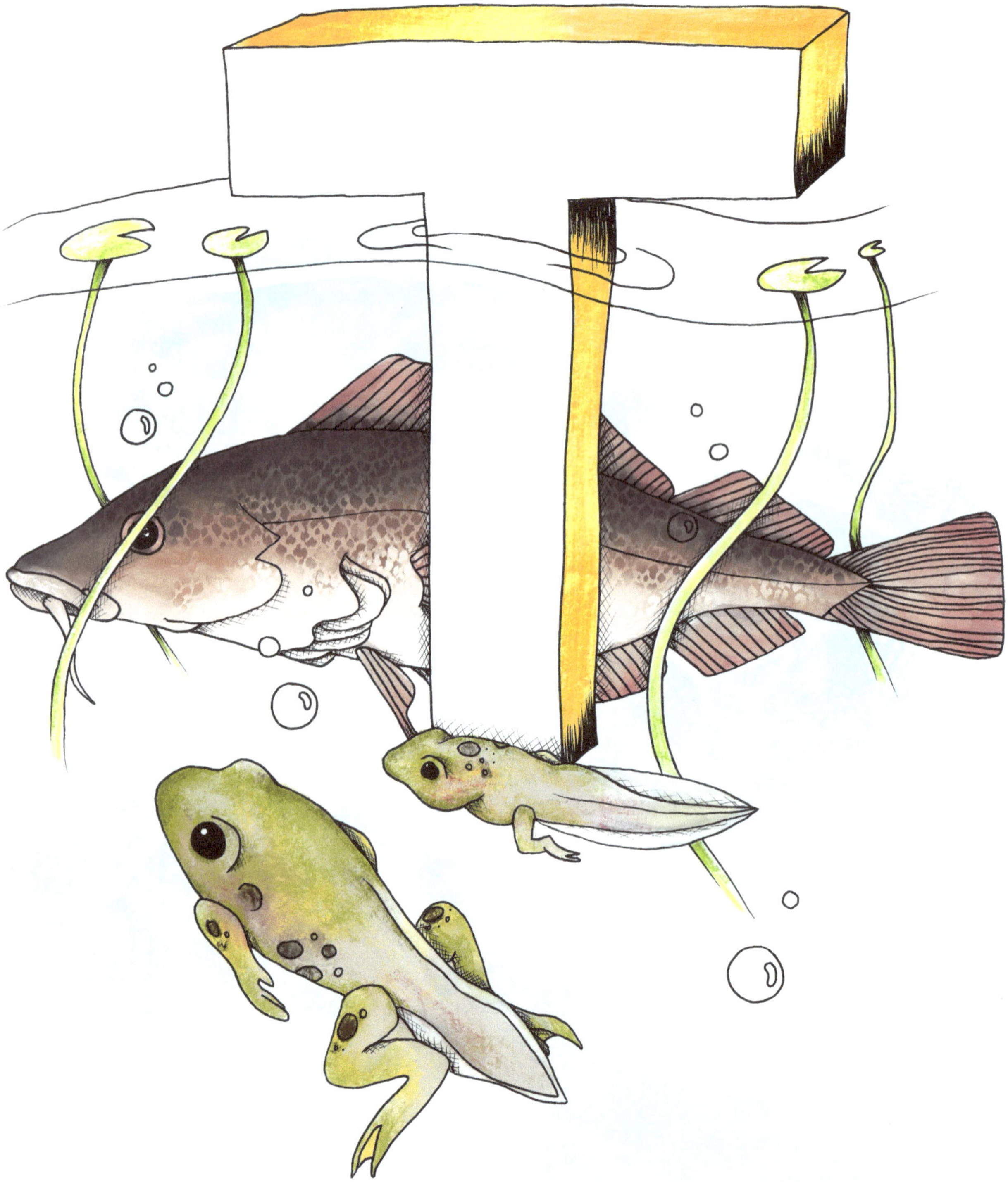

The Tadpoles

Swimming in a shallow pond, between the leaves and reeds,
Were two tiny grey tadpoles, wriggling with great speed.

They always seemed in such a rush, darting here and there,
Happy in their little world, they never had a care.

Both were lads with long dark tails called Gregory & Todd,
They shared the pond with several trout and a very grumpy Cod.

One bright and sunny morning, whilst swimming behind Greg,
Todd noticed that his friend had sprouted two back legs.

It wasn't long before, Todd gained himself a pair,
And then the two were racing, faster than a hare.

As the days went past, they wanted something more,
Whilst happy with back legs, they really wanted four.

Hooray! Their wish was answered, almost straight away,
They gained a pair of front legs, in just another day.

Now the two were swimming, like little frogs with tails,
Breast-stroking back and forth, leaving frothy trails.

Next their tails were gone, disappeared without trace,
You knew that Todd was happy, by the smile upon his face.

The tadpoles had fully grown, in front of the old cod,
Both Gregory and Todd could now be called a frog.

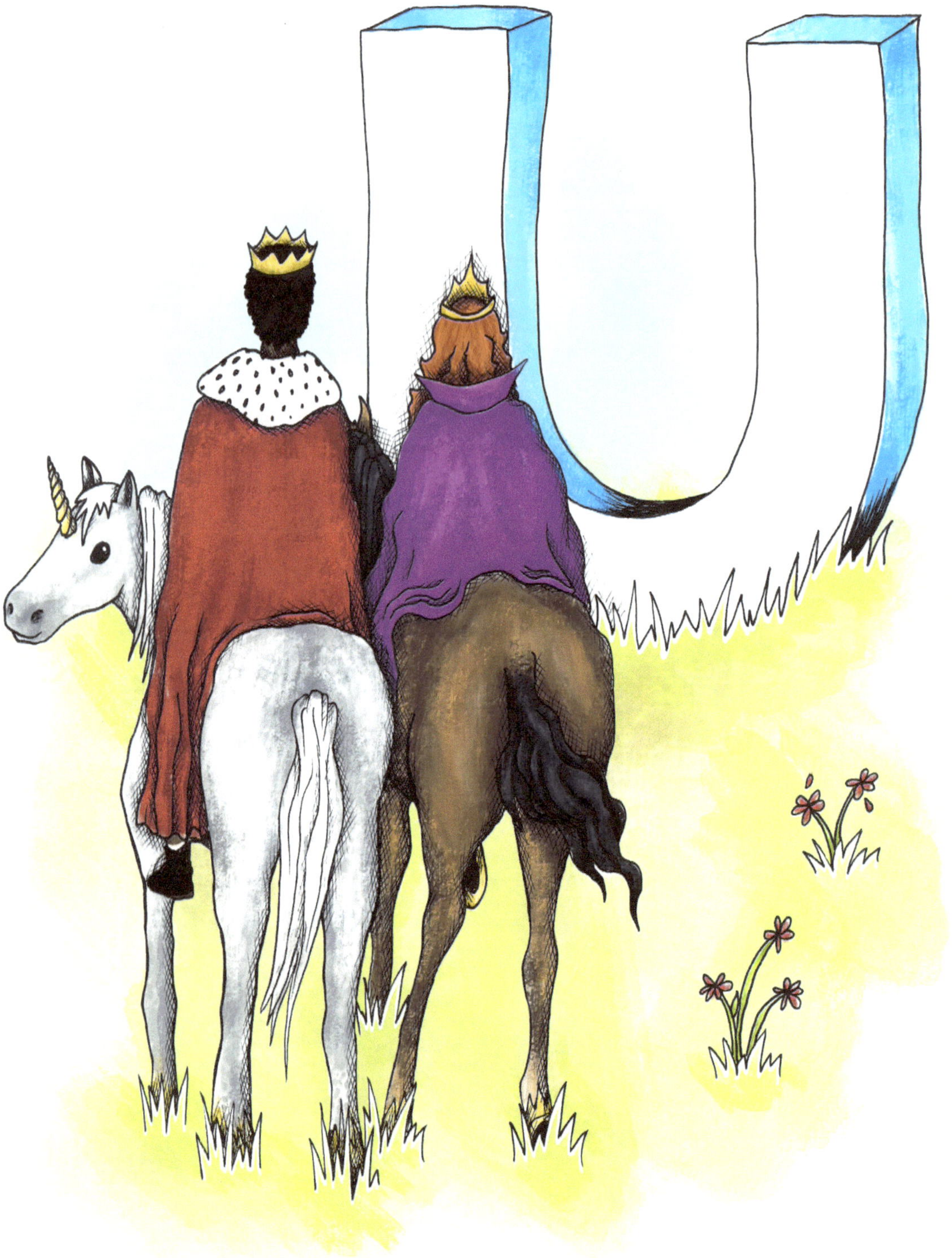

Unicorn

Once there lived in ancient times, a beast with just one horn,
A truly brilliant creature, they called a unicorn.

He was brave and handsome, with a lovely flowing mane,
With silver spots and golden hooves, 'Wonder' was his name.

The King liked to show his subjects, his majestic one horned beast,
He'd parade around on Wonder, in rain or hail or sleet.

People came from miles around, to admire clap and cheer,
They thought the king so regal, at whom to watch and peer.

Both Wonder and the King, loved to prance around with pride,
But the queen was very saddened, she had no unicorn to ride.

She wanted very much, to be high up like the king.
Yes, this would make her happy, so happy she would sing.

The King told faithful Wonder, of the problem that he faced,
Another unicorn he needed, upon which his queen could grace.

Wonder had a girlfriend, he felt sure would help him out,
He asked her very nicely, and she agreed without a doubt.

Now the King and Queen, could wander side by her side,
Waving at their subjects, and trotting stride for stride.

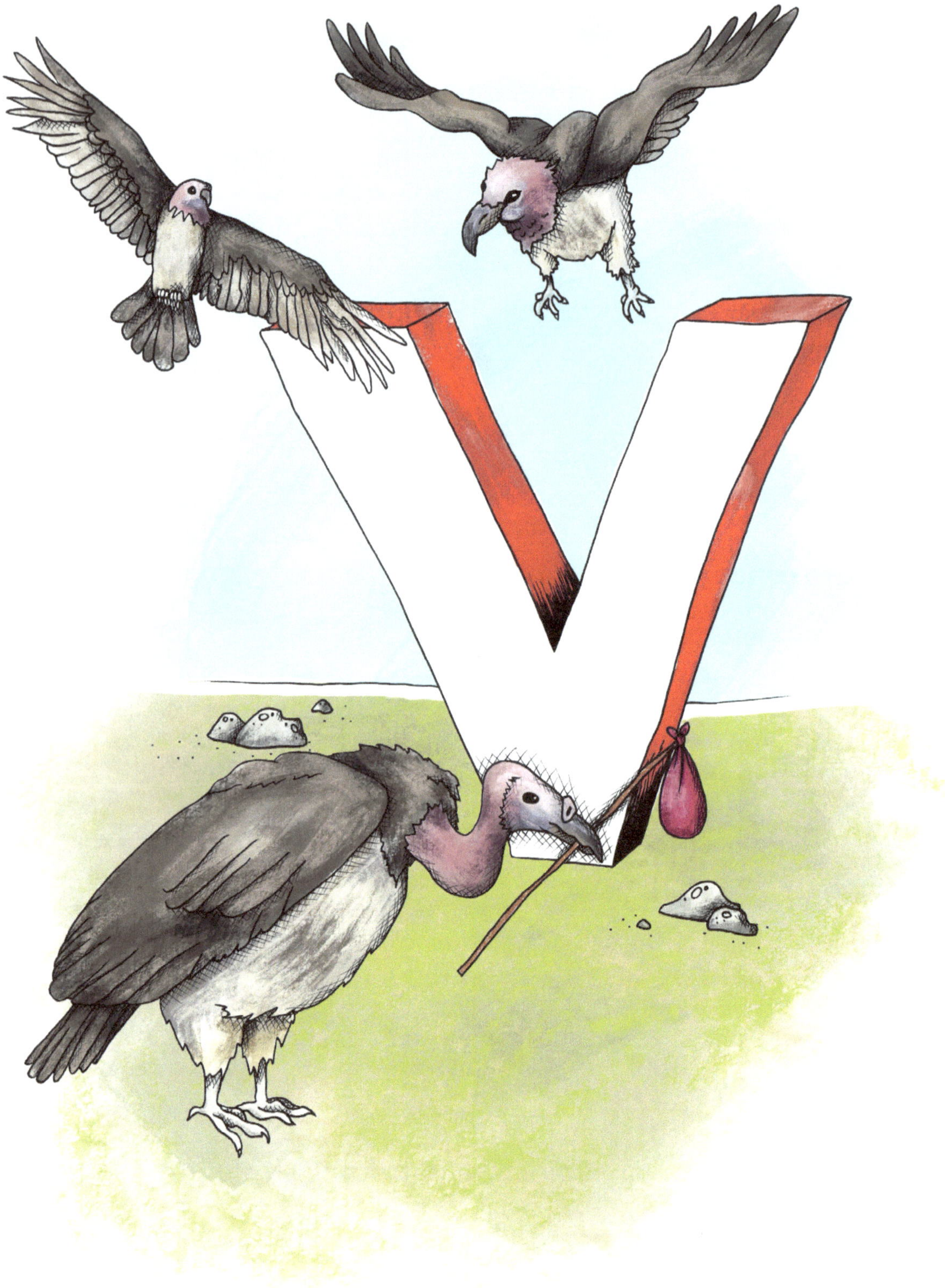

Vinnie the Vulture

Above the plains of Africa, circling round and round,
Flew a flock of vultures, looking down upon the ground.

Funny looking creatures with long and wobbly necks,
Each with a feathered collar and a nasty beak to peck.

Vinnie was the leader, a cool and trendy bird,
But he had grown tired of chasing all the herds.

He wondered what it felt like to be somebody else,
Not always feeding on, old smelly hides and pelts.

So Vinnie packed his bags and headed off alone,
Looking for adventure, away from all the bones.

First he saw some pelicans feeding in a lake,
But splashing round in water was hard for him to take.

He saw some honeysuckers, such a sweet and lively life,
Vinnie's trouble was his wings, causing lots of strife.

Next he tried to mingle, amongst the nesting storks,
Alas our little Vinnie couldn't settle in a fork.

When he saw an ostrich racing quickly 'cross the land,
Vinnie tried to keep up but got bogged down in the sand.

He cranked his neck towards the sky, so he could see above,
No one had to tell him he could never be a dove.

The other vultures called out 'You'd better think it through'
'Stick to what you're best at, the leader of our crew'

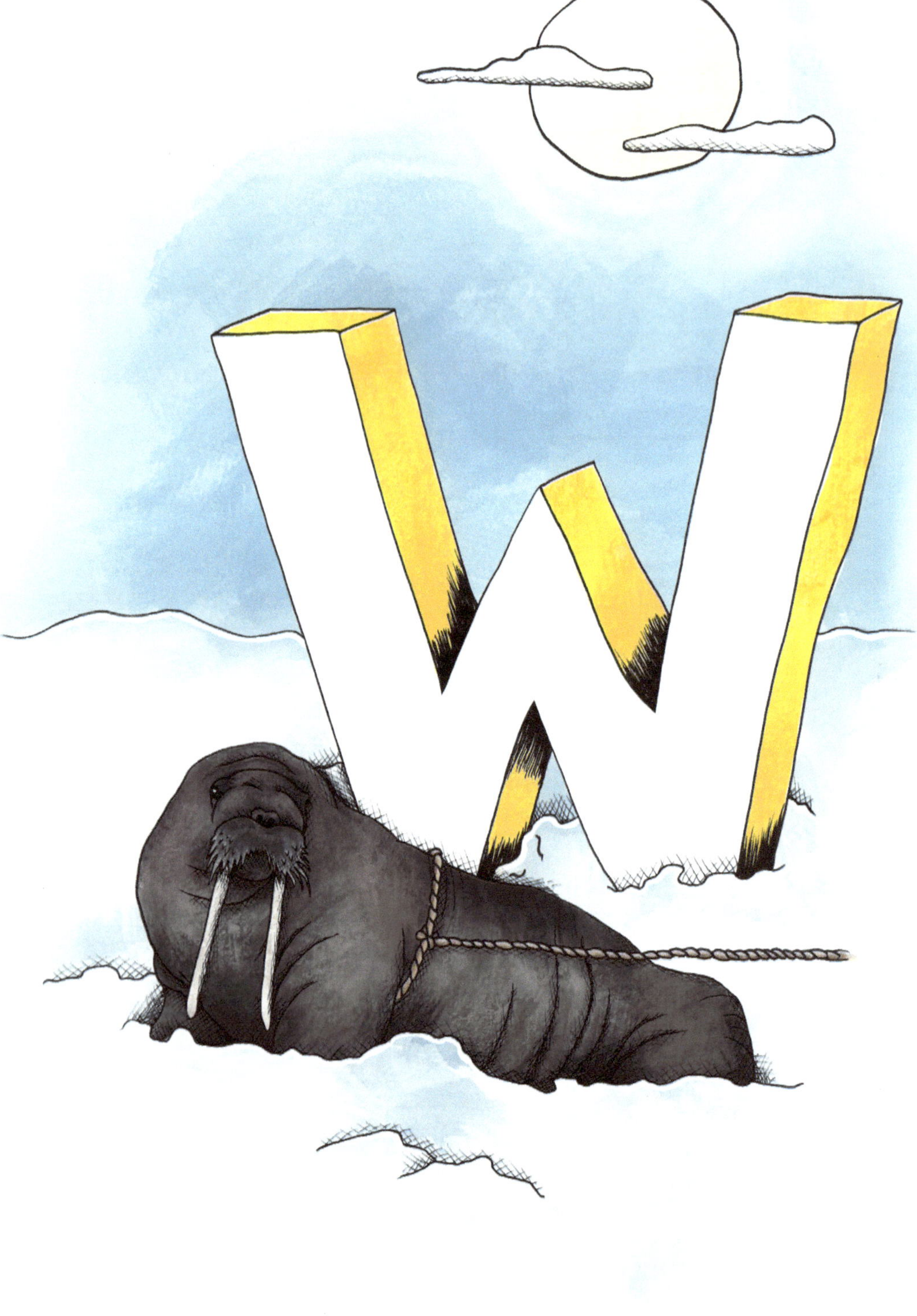

Wally the Walrus

When it's wet and windy, and everyone leaves the beach,
One animal remains, with two long sharp white teeth.

Wally was a Walrus, who was quite rotund and round,
No matter what the weather, he never left his ground.

His roly-poly belly kept him very nice and warm,
Even through the bleakest, darkest looking storm.

One lovely sunny morning, when it was not so cold,
They had a competition, all creatures vying for the gold.

The penguins, seals and killer whales all lined up to race,
Swimming through the ocean with utmost style and grace.

From upon the shore watched Wally, resting on his side,
He thought it far too energetic, to swim against the tide.

The gulls flew down by Wally, making ever such a din,
They encouraged him to enter the tug o'war to win.

Lined up against them, were seven muscly looking seals,
Whilst the gulls were only small, they were full of pep and zeal.

They tied the rope round Wally, then waited for the start,
Wings clasping on so tightly, standing just apart.

The whistle blew and off they went, pulling with such might,
The seals were strong and stretched the rope till it was really tight.

They tried and tried but could not budge, Wally from his spot,
Against his weight they soon became very tired and hot.

The seals were now exhausted, from all the work they'd done,
They all fell down together, so the little gulls had won.

News of the win spread about, to creatures of the deep,
But when they came to say 'well done', Wally was asleep.

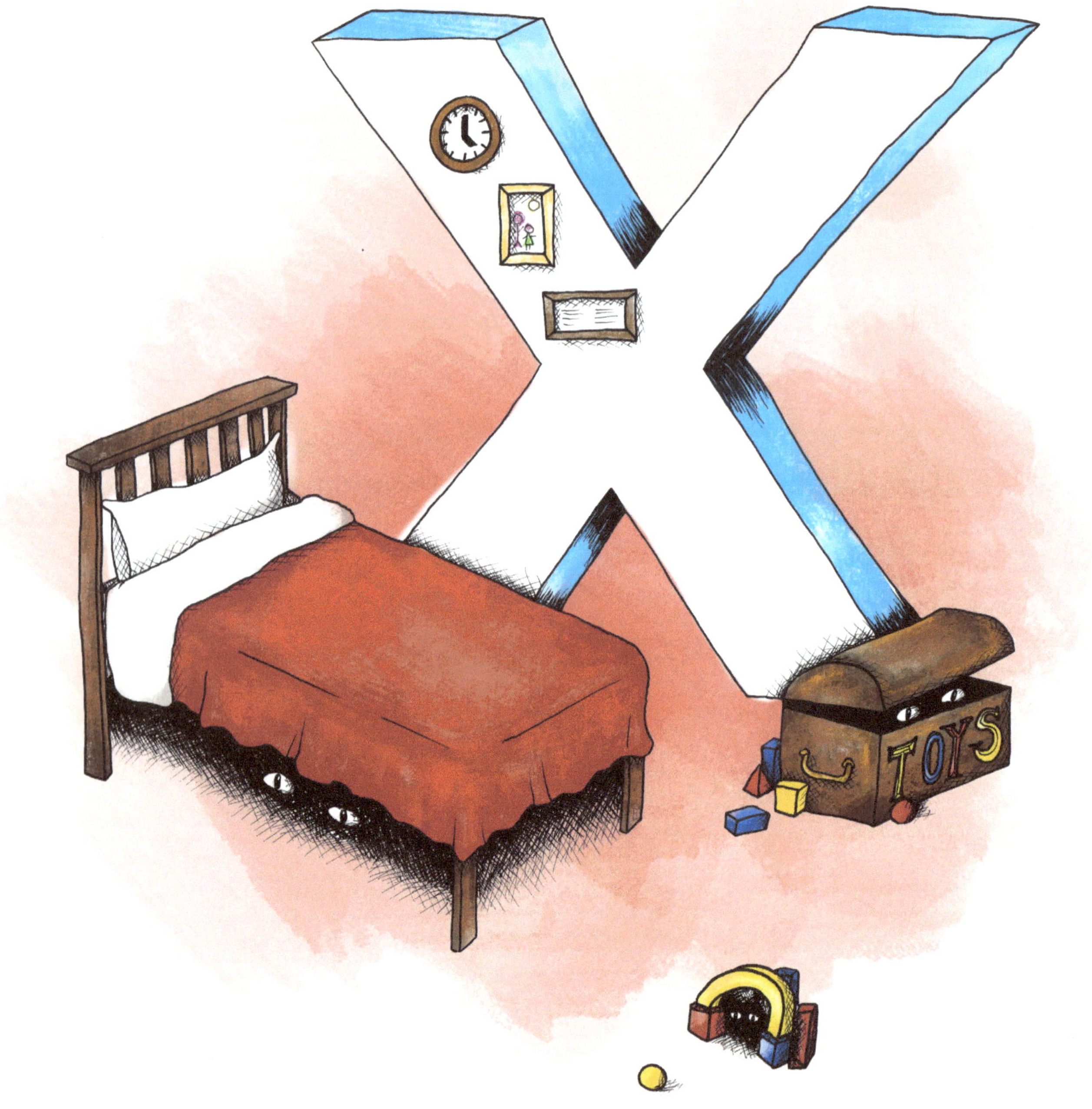
TOYS

The creature called X

X is a creature who is so hard to see,
He lives in such places as Zeberdeezee.

Clattering loudly in the cupboards each night,
Waiting in darkness to give you a fright.

At the end of the hall, or under your bed,
You're never quite sure, if he'll raise his head.

In Churdyferd City and Shakundee as well,
X likes to play with, his big noisy bell.

All the noises you hear, when you're alone,
Are usually X just having a groan.

He likes to remain in the dark out of sight,
But scampers off quickly when you turn on the light.

If your windows or doors let out a shrill noise,
It's probably X just squeezing your toys.

He's not really scary he's just very shy,
X frightens us all but do you know why?

We imagine such terrors or horrible things,
Of nasty big talons, sharp teeth and black wings.

It's easy to change him, to be fluffy and kind,
Because after all, he just lives in your mind.

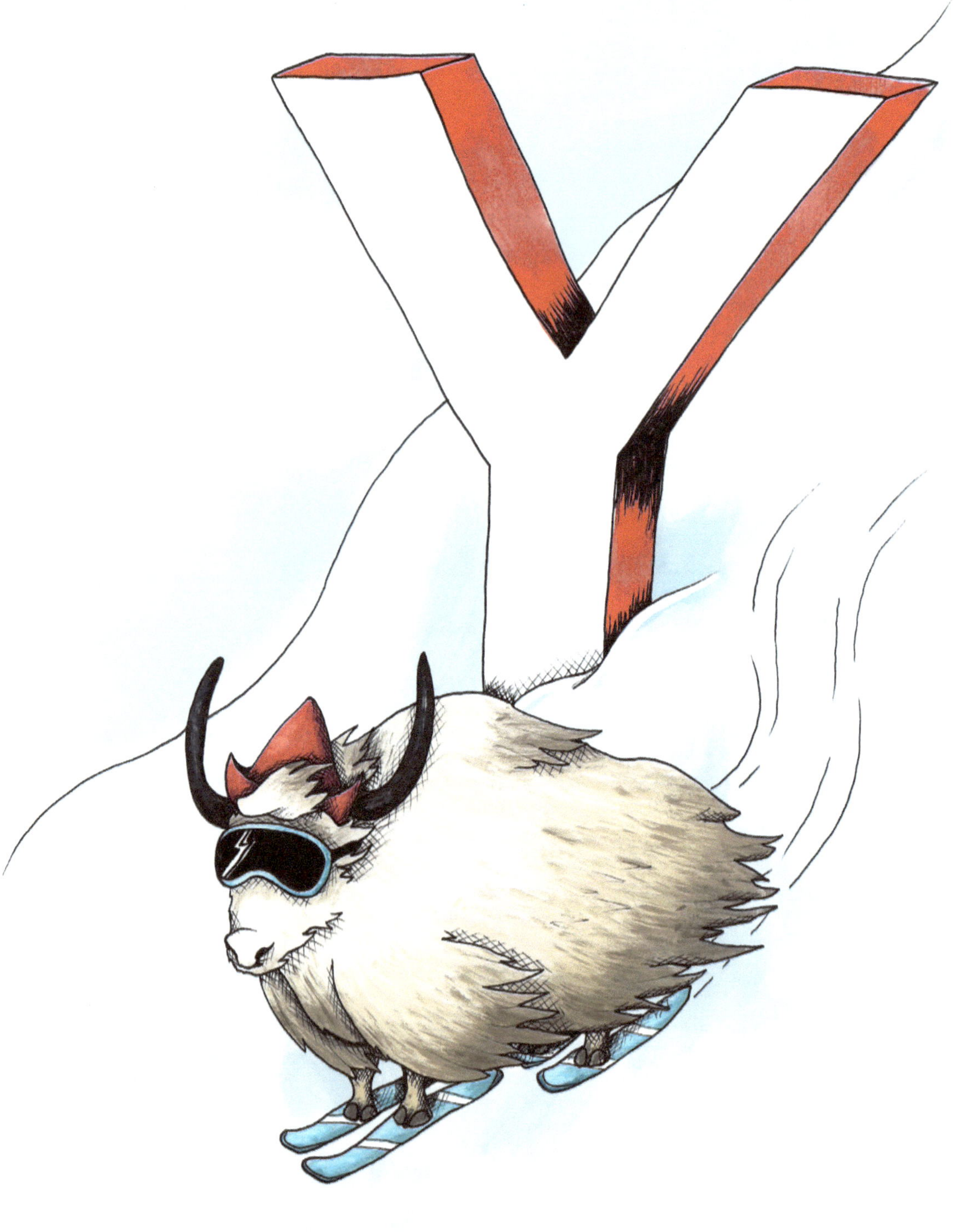

Yacky the Yak

Up in the snowy mountains, lives a very friendly fellow,
He loved to talk and chat, and roar and shout and bellow.

Yacky was a hairy yak, quite distinguished with his talking,
But when it came to travelling round, you'd never find him walking.

There was nothing Yacky enjoyed more, then discussions over tea,
So to save his breath for talking, he found it best to ski.

You'd often hear him babbling, non-stop from dusk til dawn,
Looking splendid with his hat on and glasses hanging off his horn.

Sliding down the mountainside, careful not to lose his hat,
Always eager to go faster, so he could start another chat.

He'd call on friends near and wide, to speak about the weather,
The listeners all got comfortable, in lovely seats of leather.

'Twas best to be in chairs so soft, in case he rambled on,
On more than one occasion, he went on for far too long.

Even when he found himself, with no-one else in sight,
Yacky kept on talking, into the depths of night.

So when you're in the snow, and see some deep wide tracks,
You know they might be Yacky's, the yak that loves to chat!

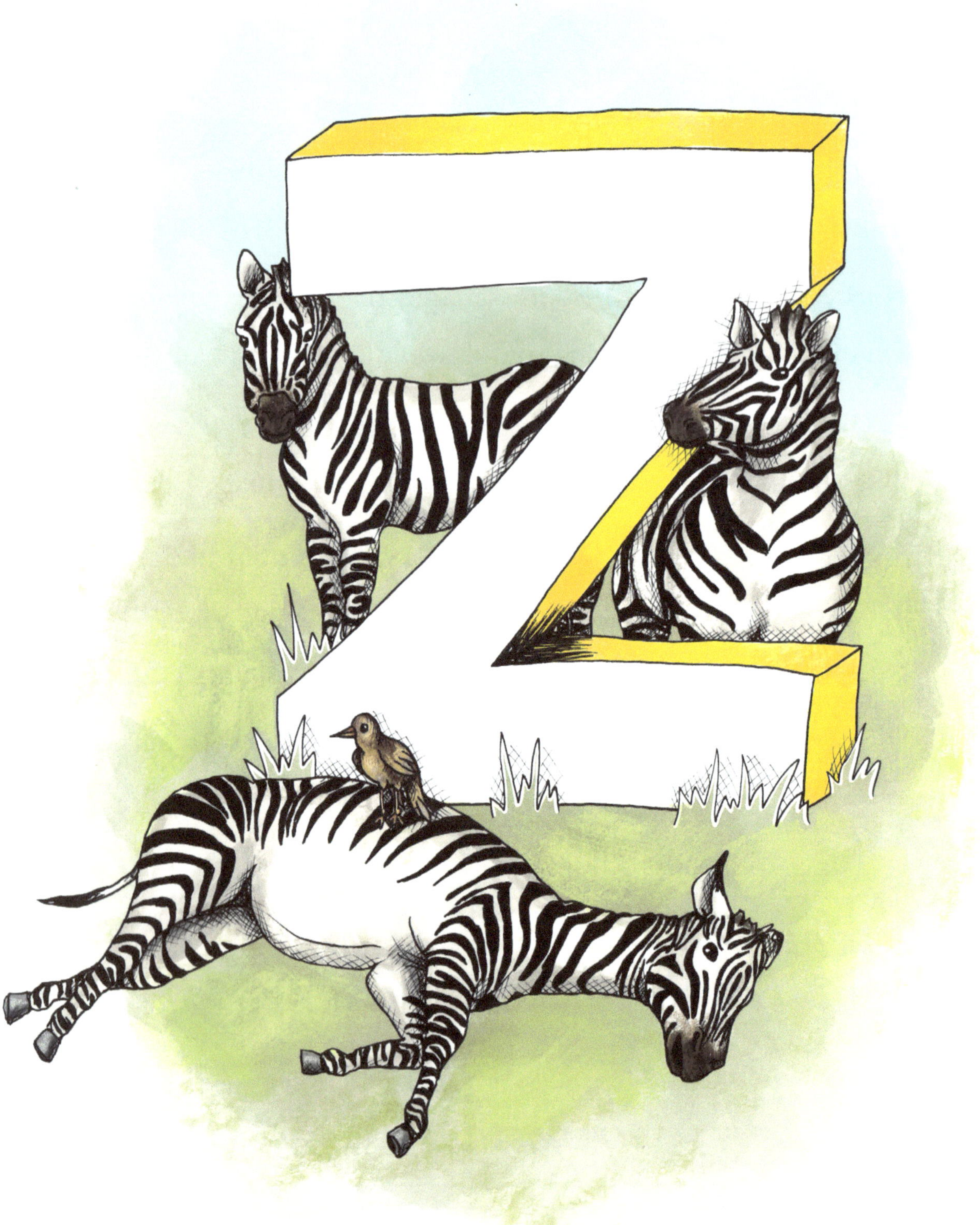

Zelda the Zebra

Zelda was a zebra, whose stripes were black and white,
But alas she had a failing, that caused her lots of strife.

When all the other zebras, were drinking at the pool,
Zelda always trotted off, to sleep where it was cool.

Soon she started snoring 'Z's, and counting lots of sheep,
It always took a mighty noise to wake her from her sleep.

If lions came in search of food, to satisfy their hunger,
The other zebras whinnied hard, and stomped their feet like thunder.

Zelda woke and looked around, then saw the lions pass,
So back she lay upon the ground, with her pillow made of grass.

Every time the lions came, whether early or quite late,
The zebras made an awful din, to try and wake their mate.

This couldn't work forever more, they had to make a deal,
They didn't want their sleepy friend to become a lion's meal.

A little bird said he could keep, the lions off the track,
If he could eat the insects, from off of Zelda's back.

He watched out for the lions, whilst sitting on her head,
And if he saw them coming, got Zelda out of bed.

Published in Australia by Sid Harta Publishers Pty Ltd,
ABN: 46 119 415 842
23 Stirling Crescent, Glen Waverley, Victoria 3150 Australia

Telephone: +61 3 9560 9920, Facsimile: +61 3 9545 1742
E-mail: author@sidharta.com.au

First published in Australia 2022, This edition published 2022
Copyright © Cam Wyllie 2022
Illustrations © Indiah Morris
Cover design, typesetting: WorkingType Studio

The right of Cam Wyllie to be identified as the Author of the Work has been asserted in accordance with the Copyright, Designs and Patents Act 1988.

All rights reserved. No part of this publication may be reproduced, stored in a retrieval system, or transmitted, in any form or by any means without the prior written permission of the publisher, nor be otherwise circulated in any form of binding or cover other than that in which it is published and without a similar condition being imposed on the subsequent purchaser.

ISBN: 978-1-925707-99-1

pp56